THE ANCIENT WISDOM OF THE STOICS:
The Art Of Harnessing The Power Of Thought

THE ANCIENT WISDOM OF THE STOICS:
The Art Of Harnessing The Power Of Thought

**James L. Jordan, PhD, PhD
and
Deovina N. Jordan, PhD, MD**

Copyright Page

Copyright © 2020 as part of "Writings: Volume Three"
James L. Jordan, PhD, PhD
and Deovina N. Jordan, PhD, MD
All Rights Reserved.

Title: THE ANCIENT WISDOM OF THE STOICS:
The Art Of Harnessing The Power Of Thought

Paperback ISBN-13: 978-1-64752-028-1
EBook ISBN-13: 978-1-64752-029-8

No portion of this book may be reproduced, stored in a retrieval system, or distributed/ transmitted in any form or by any means, whether it is electronic, mechanical, photocopying, recording, or otherwise, without the written permission of the authors and the Publisher.

Please purchase only authorized editions.

Copyright, Legal Notice, and Disclaimer

This publication is protected under the US Copyright Act of 1976 and all other applicable international, federal, state, and local laws, and all rights are reserved, including resale rights.

This book is sold subject to the condition that it shall not, by way of trade or otherwise, be lent, re-sold, hired out, or otherwise circulated without the authors' and the Publisher's prior consent, and in any form other than that in which it is published.

Although the authors and the Publisher have made every reasonable attempt to achieve complete accuracy of the content in this book, they assume no responsibility for errors or omissions.

If you have any questions about the content of this book, please contact Deja Jord, Inc.
23811 Washington Avenue, C110, #249
Murrieta, California 92562

Dedication

We dedicate this book to:

All Who Seek Wisdom

James L. Jordan, PhD, PhD

and

Deovina N. Jordan, PhD, MD

Prologue

The world is full of people who seek to be happy and wealthy in spite of the limitations that are present in their lives. Stoicism, an ancient Greek school of philosophy founded in Athens by Zeno of Citium in the early 3rd century B.C., recognized that material goods do not bring happiness. Instead, according to Stoicism, a focused, creative mind is more attuned with true wealth.

Stoic philosophers came from different walks of life. Marcus Aurelius was a Roman Emperor. Seneca was a playwright and political advisor. Epictetus was a slave turned teacher. They taught people (the public, their audience, politicians, and their students) how to appreciate who and what they have in their lives. The Stoic philosophers also taught that one should live life to the fullest as death will come, but it is not the purpose of life. They also taught that it is better to practice ethics than just preach about it. Sounds familiar? Their teachings are actually the foundation of many positive thinking books popular in the world today.

These Stoic teachings can even be heard from the pulpits of many preachers today who failed to recognize that the ancient Stoic philosophers or Stoics were pagans, not Jewish nor

Christians. But Stoics left their mark on those faiths. Before the Christian era, Judaism, which based its ethics in the Greco-Roman world, managed to obtain converts. These converts did not know much about Moses and his teachings as much as they knew Stoicism. In addition, the rabbis, who were responsible for writing the Talmud, presented themselves as Stoics.

It is important to remember that the ancient Stoics were not Christians. However, this does not mean that their teachings did not impact those who became Christians. The early Christians emerged not only from a world with Judaism but also among the Greeks and Romans who were very familiar with Stoic teachings. Stoicism originated among the Greeks and spread from there. Have you ever noted that the Apostle Paul often mentioned the Jews and the Greeks in his writings? He gave respect to Jewish and Greek ideas during the formation of the early Christian church. So, since Paul knew about their way of thinking, it is possible that the Stoic philosophy influenced Paul's teachings in the New Testament.

Truly, Stoicism has had a major impact on history and upon humankind. And the influence of Stoicism lasted through the modern times since it left its mark during the early formation of Christianity. Stoicism has been linked to greater calmness, particularly with regard to things and events beyond one's control and, as a consequence, to happiness. By knowing what is in one's power to control, one can lead a more productive life and, consequently, a more meaningful and happy life. Also, by differentiating what one can control versus what one cannot, one can be more focused in life, permitting one to do the greatest good during one's lifetime. Moreover, by knowing how to minimize negative emotions, one can maximize one's gratitude and joy in life.

Stoicism has a universal appeal. If one reads what the Stoics taught, one will see the similarities between their teachings and the teachings of Confucius and Buddha. Stoicism crosses religious faiths and cultures. In multicultural societies, people often borrow ideas from other cultures. That becomes apparent when one reads the proverbs of other cultures. Elements of Stoicism are often readily seen in many of them.

Stoicism appears to have even reached outer space. One could almost hear Mr. Spock in Star Trek as he speaks about logic, much in the manner of a Stoic. Indeed, Stoicism has had a kind of rebirth in modern times. Many books have been written about it. But it does not take long to realize that many authors focus on a single Stoic or blend in their own version of Stoicism with the words first spoken over two millennia ago.

Indeed, there are a multitude of self-help books on the market, many of them claiming to have found something new. Their messages are anything but new; much of it is actually a re-visitation of things taught by Stoics two thousand years ago. The words may be different. But the message is basically the same. You are the result of your thoughts and you can control your thoughts. It is time to reevaluate where those ideas came from, give credit where credit is due as well as develop those ideas in one's life.

This book focuses on what the ancient Stoics actually said. The topics are arranged alphabetically. The sources of the different teachings/ sayings/ statements (the 15 Stoic philosophers) are presented in the appendix. Their materials are indicated by the numbers in brackets that follow the teachings/ sayings/ statements.

Finally, this is a book without commentary by the authors. As such, the authors made no attempt to modify what the Stoics said or how they said it. That kind of commentary is left to the reader who can then use the teachings/ sayings/ statements in the book for his/ her own benefit and self-discovery.

Table of Contents

THEMES	PAGES
Section I: Actions	1
Section II: Adversity	5
Section III: Age	8
Section IV: Anger	11
Section V: Behavior	16
Section VI: Blame	19
Section VII: Character	23
Section VIII: Death	26
Section IX: Desire	32
Section X: Education/ Learning	37
Section XI: Fate/ Destiny	40
Section XII: Fear	44

Section XIII: Folly	47
Section XIV: Freedom	50
Section XV: Happiness	54
Section XVI: Judgment	59
Section XVII: Life/ Living	63
Section XVIII: Misfortune	69
Section XIX: Peace	72
Section XX: Righteousness	75
Section XXI: Self-Discipline/ Self-Control	78
Section XXII: Self-Improvement	82
Section XXIII: Speech	86
Section XXIV: Thinking	90
Section XXV: Time	94
Section XXVI: Truth	97
Section XXVII: Vanity	99

Section XXVIII: Virtue	**101**
Section XXIX: Wealth/ Riches	**105**
Section XXX: Wisdom	**109**
Section XXXI: Wisdom And Folly	**113**
Section XXXII: Wrongs/ Mistakes	**116**
Appendix: The Stoic Philosophers	**119**
About The Authors	**122**
About The Book	**124**
Books And Articles Written By The Authors	**127**

SECTION I

Actions

1.01 You have to build your life yourself - action by action. [10]
1.02 Let every action aim solely at the common good. [10]
1.03 He who pays no attention to what his neighbor does, says or thinks, preferring to concentrate on making his own actions appropriate and justifiable, uses his time better. [10]
1.04 An action will not be appropriate unless the will is honorable; for the will is from whence the action is derived. [9]
1.05 Again, the will won't be honorable unless the disposition of the mind is righteous; for from thence comes the will. [9]
1.06 Nothing should be done without a purpose. [10]
2.01 Nothing is worth doing pointlessly. [10]
2.02 Never act without purpose and resolve, or without the means to finish the job. [10]
2.03 Lay hold of today's task, and you will not depend so much upon tomorrow's task. [9]
2.04 Do what you should, not what you may. [9]
2.05 Do everything as if someone is watching you. [7]

2.06   Do everything as in the eye of another. [9]
3.01   If you do the task before you - always adhering to strict reason with zeal and energy and yet with humanity, disregarding all lesser ends and keeping the divinity within you pure and upright, as though you were even now faced with its recall - if you hold steadily to this, staying for nothing and shrinking from nothing, only seeking in each passing action a conformity with nature and in each word and utterance a fearless truthfulness, then the good life shall be yours. [10]
3.02   And from this course, no man has the power to hold you back. [10]
4.01   There are things that are within our power, and things that fall outside our power. [6]
4.02   Within our power are our own opinions, aims, desires, dislikes; in sum, our own thoughts and actions. [6]
4.03   Outside our power are our physical characteristics, the class into which we were born, our reputation in the eyes of others, and honors and offices that may be bestowed on us. [6]
5.01   In a piece of embossed silverware, what is best: the silver or the workmanship? [6]
5.02   The substance of the hand is mere flesh, but what is important is the works that the hand produces. [6]
5.03   Now, appropriate actions are of three kinds: first, those relating to mere existence; secondly, those relating to existence of a particular kind; and thirdly, those that are themselves principal duties. [6]
5.04   And what are those? [6]
5.05   Fulfilling one's role as a citizen, marrying, having children, honoring God, taking care of one's parents, and, in a word, having our desires and aversions, and our motives to act

and or not to act, as each of them ought to be, in accordance with our nature. [6]

5.06   And what is our nature? [6]

5.07   To be people who are free, noble-minded, and self-respecting. [6]

5.08   For what other animal blushes; what other animal has a sense of shame? [6]

5.09   Pleasure should be subordinated to these duties as a servant, as an attendant, so as to rouse our zeal, so as to ensure that we consistently act in accord with nature. [6]

SECTION II

Adversity

1.01   Let us be brave in the face of adversity. [8]
1.02   The greater the difficulty, the greater the glory. [13]
1.03   Fire is the test of gold; adversity, of strong men. [8]
1.04   The bravest sight in the world is to see a great man struggling against adversity. [8]
1.05   The pressure of adversity does not affect the mind of the brave man. His mind is more powerful than external circumstances. [8]
2.01   Good sides to adversity are best admired at a distance. [9]
2.02   Prosperity asks for trustworthiness; adversity demands it. [9]
2.03   The good things of prosperity are to be wished; but the good things that belong to adversity are to be admired. [8]
3.01   Be wary of the man who urges an action in which he himself incurs no risk. [9]
3.02   Great men rejoice in adversity, just as brave soldiers triumph in war. [9]

3.03 The impediment to action advances action. What stands in the way becomes the way. [10]

3.04 Adversity finds, at last, the man whom she has often passed by. [9]

SECTION III

Age

1.01 Old age isn't so bad when you consider the alternatives. [12]
1.02 Life is most delightful on the downward slope. [9]
1.03 The worst thing about getting old is that evil men cease to fear you. [9]
2.01 To live long, live unhurriedly. [13]
2.02 You will become an old man in good time if you wish to be an old man before your time. [10]
3.01 As for old age, embrace and love it. It abounds with pleasure if you know how to use it. [8]
3.02 The gradually declining years are among the sweetest in a man's life, and I maintain that because even when they have reached the extreme limit, they still have their indulgences. [8]
3.03 No one is so old that he does not think he could live another year. [13]
4.01 We must take care to live not merely a long life, but a full one; for living a long life requires only good fortune, but living a full life requires character. [9]

4.02   Long is the life that is fully lived; it is fulfilled only when the mind supplies its own good qualities and empowers itself from within. [9]

4.03   Not how long, but how well you have lived is the main thing. [8]

4.04   Men do not care how nobly they live but only how long, although it is within the reach of every man to live nobly but within no man's power to live long. [9]

5.01   The best armor of old age is a well spent life; a life employed in the pursuit of useful knowledge, in honorable actions and the practice of virtue; in which he who labors to improve himself from his youth, will in age reap the happiest fruits of them; not only because these never leave a man, not even in the most extreme old age; but because a conscience bearing witness that our life was well-spent, together with the remembrance of past good actions, yields an unspeakable comfort to the soul. [13]

6.01   Old age has deformities enough of its own. One should never add to them the deformity of vice. [11]

6.02   There is nothing more despicable than an old man who has no other proof of his having lived long in this world but his old age. [8]

SECTION IV

Anger

1.01   Anger often comes to us, but more often we come to it. [9]
1.02   Anger, though concealed, is betrayed by one's expression. [9]
1.03   The anger that is not deserved is one that lasts up to two days. [9]
2.01   Anger is like those ruins which smash themselves on where they fall. [8, 9]
2.02   The entire world would perish, if pity does not limit anger. [9]
3.01   An angry man opens his mouth and shuts his eyes. [11]
3.02   Anger so clouds the mind that it cannot perceive the truth. [11]
3.03   In anger, nothing right or judicious can be done. [13]
3.04   So much worse are the consequences of anger than its causes. [10]
4.01   Do you desire not to be angry? [9]
4.02   Do not be inquisitive. [9]

4.03 He who inquires what is said of him only works out his own misery. [9]
4.04 To alleviate anger, do not feed it. [6]
4.05 Say to yourself: I used to be angry every day; then every other day; now only every third or fourth day. [6]
4.06 When you reach thirty days of anger, offer a sacrifice of thanksgiving to God. [6]
4.07 Hesitation is the best cure for anger. [9]
4.08 The first blows of anger are heavy, but if one waits, one will reconsider. [9]
5.01 Whenever you are angry, be assured that it is not only a present evil, but that you have worsened a habit. [6]
5.02 As long as you honor material things, direct your anger at yourself rather than the thief or adulterer. [6]
5.03 Run down the list of those who felt intense anger at something: the most famous, the most unfortunate, the most hated, the most whatever. [10]
5.04 Where is all that now? [10]
5.05 Smoke, dust, legend...or not even a legend. [10]
5.06 Think of all the examples. [10]
5.07 And how trivial the things we want so passionately. [10]
5.08 The deferring of anger is the best antidote to anger. [8]
6.01 Any person capable of angering you becomes your master; he can anger you only when you permit yourself to be disturbed by him. [6]
6.02 If a person gave your physical body to any stranger he encountered, you would certainly be angry. [6]
6.03 And do you feel no shame in letting your own mind be confused and mystified by anyone who happens to verbally attack you? [6]

7.01   Why are we not angry if we are told that we have a headache, and why are we angry if we are told that we reason badly, or choose wrongly? [6]

7.02   The reason is that we are quite certain if we do not have a headache, or are not lame, but we are not so sure if we made the correct choice. [6]

7.03   So, we have assurance only because we see with our whole sight but it puts us in suspense and surprise when another sees the opposite with his whole sight, and still more so when a thousand others deride our choice. [6]

7.04   For we must prefer our own lights to those of so many others, and that is bold and difficult. [6]

8.01   The greatest remedy for anger is delay. [8]

8.02   When you are offended at any man's fault, turn to yourself and study your own failings. [6]

8.03   Then you will forget your anger. [6]

8.04   When you are annoyed at someone's mistake, immediately look at yourself and reflect on how you also fail; for example, in thinking that good equals money, or pleasure, or a bit of fame. [10]

8.05   By being mindful of this you'll quickly forget your anger, especially if you realize that the person was under stress, and could do little else. [10]

8.06   And, if you can, find a way to alleviate that stress. [10]

9.01   Why should we feel anger at the world? [10]

9.02   As if the world would notice? [10]

9.03   Our anger and annoyance are more detrimental to us than the things themselves which anger or annoy us. [10]

9.04   Anger: an acid that can do more harm to the vessel in which it is stored than to anything on which it is poured. [8]

9.05 How much more grievous are the consequences of anger than its causes. [10]

9.06 Anger, if not restrained, is frequently more hurtful to us than the injury that provokes it. [8]

10.01 Say to yourself in the early morning: Today, I shall meet ungrateful, violent, treacherous, envious, uncharitable men. [10]

10.02 All of these things have come upon them through their ignorance of real good and bad. [10]

10.03 I can neither be harmed by any of them, for no man will involve me in wrong, nor can I be angry with my kinsman or hate him; for we have come into the world to work together. [10]

SECTION V

Behavior

1.01 Most of what we say and do are not essential. [10]
1.02 If you can eliminate them, you'll have more time, and more tranquility. [10]
1.03 Ask yourself at every moment: Is this necessary? [10]
1.04 What are we to do, then? [6]
1.05 To make the best of what lies within our power, deal with everything else as it comes. [6]
1.06 How does it come then? [6]
1.07 As God wills. [6]
1.08 Then cultivate these, for they are wholly within your power: sincerity, dignity, industriousness, and sobriety. [10]
1.09 Avoid grumbling; be frugal, considerate, and frank; be temperate in manner and speech; carry yourself with authority. [10]
1.10 Be firm or mild as the occasion may require. [11]
1.11 You should banish any thoughts of how you may appear to others. [10]

1.12   Don't you know that a good man does nothing for appearance sake, but for the sake of having done right? [6]
2.01   Remember that you ought to behave in life as you would at a banquet. [6]
2.02   As food is being passed around and it comes to you, be polite, stretch out your hand and take a portion of it. [6]
2.03   Then pass it on. Do not keep it. [6]
2.04   Or if it has not come to you yet, do not project your eagerness to get food, but wait until it comes in front of you. [6]
2.05   So, act appropriately toward children. Do the same toward women, politicians, and other people. [6]
3.01   Don't concern yourself with another person's business. [6]
3.02   It is his problem if he receives you badly. [6]
3.03   And you cannot suffer for another person's fault. So don't worry about his behavior. [6]
4.01   Those people who are serious in trivial matters will be unreasonable in serious matters. [11]
4.02   The lightheartedness of behavior is the bane of all that is good and virtuous. [9]
4.03   Good-breeding is the art of showing men, by external signs, the internal regard we have for them. [12]
4.04   It also arises from good sense and improved by keeping good company. [12]

SECTION VI

Blame

1.01   An uneducated person will lay the fault of his own bad decisions upon others. [6]
1.02   Someone who is just starting with his education will lay the fault on himself. [6]
1.03   Someone who is perfectly educated will blame neither others nor himself. [6]
1.04   Small-minded people blame others. [6]
1.05   Average people blame themselves. [6]
1.06   The wise see all blame as foolishness. [6]
2.01   Never praise or blame people on common grounds; look at their judgements exclusively. [6]
2.02   Because that is the determining factor, which makes everyone's actions either good or bad. [6]
2.03   Whatever one blames in the other person, he will find it in his own heart. [9]
2.04   Therefore, when we are hindered, or disturbed, or grieved, let us not attribute it to others but to ourselves; that is, to our own principles. [6]

3.01   When you are feeling upset, angry, or sad, don't blame another person for your state of mind. [6]
3.02   Your condition is the result of your own opinions and interpretations. [6]
3.03   If you choose, you are free; if you choose, therefore, you need not blame or accuse anybody. [6]
3.04   All things will be according to your mind and according to the Mind of God. [6]
3.05   Remember then that if you think the things which are by nature free and think the things which are in the power of others to be your own, you will be hindered, you will lament, you will be disturbed, you will blame both gods and men: but if you think only about that which is your own to be your own, and if you think about that which is another's, as it really is - belonging to another, no man will ever compel you, no man will hinder you, you will never blame any man, you will accuse no man, you will do nothing against your will, no man will harm you, you will have no enemy, for you will not suffer any harm. [6]
3.06   Teach yourself that for the same things you blame others, you also blame yourself. [5]
4.01   When another blames you or hates you, or people voice similar criticisms, go to their souls, penetrate inside and see what sort of people they are. [10]
4.02   You will realize that there is no need to be tormented with anxiety that they should hold any particular opinion about you. [10]
4.03   If it is in your control, why do you do it? [10]
4.04   If it's in someone else's control, then who are you blaming? Atoms? The gods? It is stupid either way. [10]
4.05   Blame no one. [10]

4.06 Set people straight, if you can. [10]
4.07 If you cannot, just repair the damage. [10]
5.01 In the long run, every man will pay the penalty for his own misdeeds. [6]
5.02 The man who remembers this will be angry with no one, indignant with no one, revile no one, blame no one, offend no one, hate no one. [6]
5.03 When you are feeling upset, angry, or sad, don't blame another for your state of mind. [6]
5.04 Your condition is the result of your own opinions and interpretations. ... [6]
5.05 When anyone provokes you, remember that it is actually your own opinion provoking you. [6]
5.06 It is not the person who insults you or attacks you who torments your mind, but the view you take of these things. [6]

SECTION VII

Character

1.01   Yet living and dying, honor and dishonor, pain and pleasure, riches and poverty, and so forth are equally the lot of good men and bad. [10]
1.02   Things like these neither elevate nor degrade; and, therefore, they are no more good than they are evil. [10]
1.03   The good of man, and likewise his ill, lies in how he exercises his choice, while everything else is nothing to us. [6]
1.04   The nobler a man, the harder it is for him to suspect inferiority in others. [13]
2.01   Your mind will take on the character of your most frequent thoughts: souls are dyed by thoughts. [10]
2.02   Don't let it be true that you have an ill/bad character. [10]
2.03   If anybody reports you as not an honest man, let your practice show others the lie. [10]
2.04   This is the mark of a perfect character - to pass through each day as though it were the last, without agitation, without indolence, and without pretense. [10]

3.01   A man's manner and character is what most defines him. [13]
3.02   Hesitancy leads to uncertain outcomes. [6]
3.03   Therefore, give yourself fully to your endeavors. [6]
3.04   Decide to build your character through excellent actions and you will attain worthy goals. [6]
3.05   The trials you encounter will increase your strengths. [6]
3.06   Remain steadfast...and one day you will build something that endures: something worthy of your potential. [6]
4.01   We must consider when is the time for singing, when is the time for playing, and in whose presence: what will be unsuitable to the occasion; whether our companions will despise us or we will despise ourselves: when to jest, and whom to mock: and on what occasion to be conciliatory and to whom: in other words, how one ought to maintain one's character in society. [6]
4.02   Whenever you deviate from any of these principles, you suffer loss; not loss from without, but loss from within - due to the very act itself. [6]
4.03   Our character is not so much the product of race and heredity as of those circumstances by which nature forms our habits, by which we are nurtured and by which we live.[13]
5.01   Taking account of the value of externals, you see, comes at some cost to the value of one's own character. [6]
5.02   You can tell the character of every man when you see how he receives praise. [9]
5.03   No one can hide behind a mask for too long; the pretense soon lapses into the true character. [9]

SECTION VIII

Death

1.01 Why are you afraid of death? [7]
1.02 Where you are, death is not. [7]
1.03 Where death is, you are not. [7]
1.04 What is it that you fear? [7]
1.05 Stop whatever you're doing for a moment and ask yourself: Am I afraid of death because I won't be able to do this anymore? [10]
1.06 Death is the separation of the soul from the body. [3]
1.07 No evil is honorable: but death is honorable; therefore, death is not evil. [15]
1.08 The act of dying is one of the acts of life. [10]
1.09 The final hour when we cease to exist does not itself bring death; in and of itself, it merely completes the death-process. [8]
1.10 We reach death at that moment, but we have been a long time on the way. [8]
1.11 We are wrong in looking forward to death: in great measure, it is past already. [9]

2.01 [Death is] a punishment to some, to some a gift, and to many a favor. [8]
2.02 Death is the wish of some, the relief of many, and the end of all. [8]
2.03 It is not death or pain that is to be dreaded, but the fear of pain or death. [6]
2.04 It is our attitude towards events, not the events themselves, which we can control. [6]
2.05 Nothing is, by its own nature, calamitous - even death is terrible only if we fear it. [6]
2.06 For it is not death or pain that is to be feared, but the fear of pain or death. [6]
2.07 If death causes you no pain when you're dead, it is foolish to allow the fear of it to cause you pain now. [7]
2.08 It is not death that a man should fear, but he should fear never beginning to live. [10]
2.09 After death, there is nothing. [9]
3.01 Death is the discharge of our debt of sorrow. [9]
3.02 Death is a release from the impressions of the senses, and from desires that make us their puppets, and from the vagaries of the mind, and from the hard service of the flesh. [10]
3.03 He who fears death either fears the loss of sensation or a different kind of sensation. [10]
3.04 But, if you shall have no sensation, neither will you feel any harm; and if you shall acquire another kind of sensation, you will be a different kind of living being and you will not cease to live .[10]
4.01 Do not expect good from another person's death. [12]
4.02 Do not grudge your brother his rest. [9]

4.03   He has, at last, become free, safe and immortal, and he is joyful to go to boundless heavens; he has left this earthly place and has soared upwards to that place which receives in its happy bosom the souls set free from the chains of matter. [9]

4.04   Your brother has not lost the light of day, but has obtained a more enduring light. [9]

4.05   He has not left us, but has gone on before. [9]

5.01   Most men ebb and flow in wretchedness between the fear of death and the hardship of life; they are unwilling to live, and yet they do not know how to die. [8]

5.02   Add to each day something to fortify you against poverty and death. [8]

5.03   It is unknown the place and uncertain the time where death awaits you; thus, you must expect death to find you at any time and at any place. [9]

5.04   Our life is our own today; tomorrow we will be dust, a shade, and a tale. [2]

5.05   Live mindful of death; the hour flies. [2]

5.06   Do not act as if you were going to live ten thousand years. [10]

5.07   Death hangs over you. While you live, while it is in your power, be good. [10]

5.08   Death smiles at us all; all a man can do is smile back. [10]

6.01   Do not fear death, but welcome it, since it too comes from nature. [10]

6.02   For just as we are young and grow old, and flourish and reach maturity, have teeth and a beard and grey hairs, conceive, become pregnant, and bring forth new life, and all the other natural processes that follow the seasons of our existence, so also do we have death. [10]

6.03   A thoughtful person will never take death lightly, impatiently, or scornfully, but will wait for it as one of life's natural processes. [10]
6.04   A man afraid of death will never play the part of a live man. [9]
6.05   Such is the blindness, nay the insanity, of mankind that some men are driven to death by the fear of it. [9]
7.01   Death is nothing to us: since when we are ready, death has not come, and when death has come, we are not ready. [7]
7.02   Death is nothing to us: for after our bodies have been dissolved by death, they are without sensation, and that which lacks sensation is nothing to us. [7]
7.03   And, therefore, a right understanding of death makes mortality enjoyable, not because it adds an infinite span of time, but because it takes away the craving for immortality. [7]
7.04   Dead, we become the lumber of the world. And to that mass of matter, we shall be swept, where things destroyed with things unborn are kept. [9]
8.01   Death does not concern us, because as long as we exist, death is not here. And when it does come, we no longer exist. [7]
8.02   Death is meaningless to the living because they are alive, and meaningless to the dead … because they are dead. [7]
9.01   Refuse to let the thought of death bother you: nothing is grim when we have escaped that fear. [9]
9.02   It is not death we fear, but the thought of it. [8]
9.03   Accustom yourself to believing that death is nothing to us, for good and evil imply awareness, and death is the deprivation of all awareness; therefore understanding that death is nothing to us makes life enjoyable, not by adding an

unlimited time to life, but by taking away the yearning for immortality. [7]

9.04   For life is not fearsome for those who thoroughly comprehend that there is no fear in stopping to live. [7]

9.05   He who fears death has already lost the life he covets. [11]

SECTION IX

Desire

1.01 Men seek retreats for themselves such as houses in the country, sea-shores, and mountains; and you, too, are accustomed to desire such things. [10]
1.02 But this is altogether a mark of the most common sort of men, for it is in your power whenever you shall choose to retreat or withdraw. [10]
1.03 For nowhere, either with a quieter state or more freedom from trouble, does a man retire than into his own soul? [10]
1.04 Don't you want to be free of all that? But how can you do it? You have often heard how - you need to stop the desire completely and train yourself to dislike the things that you cannot have. [6]
1.05 You should dissociate yourself from everything outside yourself - the body, possessions, reputation, books, applause, as well as office or lack of office. [6]
1.06 A preference for any of them makes you a slave or a subordinate, and prone to disappointment. [6]
1.07 No one can have all that he desires. [9]

1.08 Let your desires be ruled by reason. [13]
2.01 The thirst of desire is never filled, nor fully satisfied. [13]
2.02 Nothing is sufficient for the person who finds sufficiency too little. [7]
2.03 He who does not find a little enough will find nothing enough. [7]
2.04 Nothing is enough for the man to whom enough is too little. [7]
2.05 Covetousness like jealousy, when it has taken root, never leaves a person, but is with him for life. [6]
2.06 Cowardice is the dread of what will happen. [6]
3.01 Never value anything as profitable to yourself which shall compel you to break your promise, to lose your self-respect, to hate any man, to suspect, to curse, to act as hypocrite, to desire anything which needs walls and curtains. [10]
3.02 That moderation which nature prescribes, which limits our desires by resources restricted to our needs, has abandoned the field; it has now come to this - that to want only what is enough is a sign both of boorishness and of utter destitution. [8]
3.03 Not what we have but what we enjoy that constitutes our abundance. [7]
4.01 Keep the prospect of death, exile and all such apparent tragedies before you every day - especially death - and you will never have an abject thought, or desire anything in excess. [6]
4.02 Destroy desire completely for the present. [6]
4.03 For if you desire anything which is not in your power, you will be unfortunate. [6]

4.04   Let us train our minds to desire what the situation demands. [8]
4.05   The things you really need are few and easy to come by; but the things you can imagine you need are infinite, and you will never be satisfied. [7]
4.06   Protect what belongs to you at all costs; do not desire what belongs to another. [6]
5.01   The greatest wealth is a poverty of desires. [9]
5.02   He is a king who fears nothing; he is a king who desires nothing! [8]
5.03   We are at the mercy of whoever wields authority over the things we either desire or detest. [6]
5.04   If you will be free, then do not wish to have, or avoid, things that other people control because then you must serve as their slave. [6]
5.05   Freedom is not procured by a full enjoyment of what is desired, but by controlling the desire. [6]
5.06   Freedom is not mastered by satisfying desire, but by eliminating desire. [6]
5.07   Freedom is not attained through the satisfaction of desires, but through the suppression of desires. [6]
6.01   Each man has his own desires; all do not possess the same inclinations. [2]
6.02   It is the privilege … of godlike men to want little. [5]
6.03   Free is the person who lives as he wishes and cannot be coerced, impeded or compelled, whose impulses cannot be thwarted, who always gets what he desires, and never has to experience what he would rather avoid. [6]
7.01   If then you desire (aim at) such great things, remember that you must not (attempt to) lay hold of them with a small effort. [6]

7.02 When you feel a burning desire for something that appears pleasurable, you are like a person under a spell. [6]
7.03 Instead of acting on impulse, take a step back - wait till the fascination fades and you can see things as they are. [6]
7.04 Let reason govern desire. [13]
7.05 Do your best to rein in your desire. [6]
7.06 For if you desire something that is not within your own control, disappointment will surely follow; meanwhile, you will be neglecting the very things that are within your control that are worthy of desire. [6]

SECTION X

Education/ Learning

1.01 The purpose of education is to free the student from the tyranny of the present. [13]
1.02 Education gives sobriety to the young, comfort to the old, riches to the poor, and ornament to the rich. [5]
1.03 Frivolity is inborn, conceit acquired by education. [13]
2.01 The foundation of every state is the education of its youth. [5]
2.02 Natural ability without education has more often raised a man to glory and virtue than education without natural ability. [10]
2.03 We learn nothing from history except that we learn nothing from history. [13]
3.01 Where there is ignorance, there is also want of learning and instruction in essentials. [6]
3.02 Let us not unlearn what we have already learned. [5]
3.03 The mind is slow to unlearn what it learnt early in life. [8]

3.04   It is impossible to begin to learn that which one thinks one already knows. [6]
3.05   A lesson that is never learned can never be too often taught. [9]
3.06   Be careful to leave your sons well instructed rather than rich, for the hopes of the instructed are better than the wealth of the ignorant. [6]
4.01   Don't just say you have read books. [6]
4.02   Show that you have learned to think better, to be a more discriminating and reflective person. [6]
4.03   Books are the training weights of the mind. [6]
4.04   They are very helpful, but it would be a bad mistake to suppose that one has made progress simply by having internalized their contents. [6]
4.05   As long as you live, learn how to live. [9]
4.06   You should keep on learning as long as there is something you do not know. [9]
5.01   Bitter are the roots of study, but sweet are their fruits. [12]
5.02   The road to learning by precept is long, but by example, short and effective. [8]

SECTION XI

Fate/ Destiny

1.01   Fate is the endless chain of causation, whereby things are; the reason or formula by which the world goes on. [15]
1.02   Fate rules the affairs of men, with no recognizable order. [8]
1.03   Events do not just happen, but arrive by appointment. [6]
1.04   Everything that happens, happens as it should. [10]
1.05   Submit to the fate of your own free will. [10]
1.06   Welcome every experience the looms of fate may weave for you. [10]
1.07   Circumstances do not rise to meet our expectations. [6]
1.08   Events happen as they do. People behave as they are. [6]
1.09   Embrace what you actually get. [6]
2.01   The great soul surrenders itself to fate. [8]
2.02   Fate guides the person who accepts it and hinders the person who resists it. [4]
2.03   Accept the things to which fate binds you, and love the people which fate brings to you, but do so with all your heart. [10]

2.04   It is not what happens to you, but how you react to it that matters. [6]

3.01   Do not seek that the things which happen should happen as you wish; but wish the things which happen to be as they are, and you will have a tranquil flow of life. [6]

3.02   How ridiculous and how strange is it to be surprised at anything which happens in life. [10]

3.03   It is possible to depart from life at this moment. [10]

3.04   Have this thought in mind whenever you act, speak, or think. [10]

3.05   Whatever may happen to you was prepared for you from all eternity; and the implication of causes was from eternity spinning the thread of your being. [10]

4.01   It is not the great soul that surrenders itself to fate, but a puny degenerate thing, that struggles. [9]

4.02   Make the best use of what is in your power, and take the rest as it happens. [6]

4.03   Everything that occurs happens as it should, and if you observe carefully, you will find this to be so. [10]

4.04   Adapt yourself to the things among which your lot has been cast and love sincerely the fellow creatures whom destiny has ordained that you shall live with. [10]

5.01   A strict belief in fate is the worst of slavery, imposing upon our necks an everlasting lord and tyrant, whom we are to stand in awe of day and night. [7]

5.02   Disease is an impediment to the body, but not to the will, unless the will, itself, chooses to do so. [6]

5.03   Lameness is an impediment to the leg, but not to the will. [6]

5.04   And add this reflection on the occasion of everything that happens; for you will find it an impediment to something else, but not to yourself. [6]

6.01   Fate leads the willing, and drags along the reluctant. [8]

6.02   Make the best use of what is in your power, and accept the rest as it happens. [6]

6.03   The time is at hand when you will have forgotten everything; and the time is at hand when all will have forgotten you. [10]

6.04   Always reflect that soon you will be no one, and nowhere. [10]

6.05   Every journey has an end. [9]

6.06   That which comes after, conforms to that which has gone before. [10]

SECTION XII

Fear

1.01 A man who causes fear cannot be free from fear. [7]
1.02 To be feared is to fear. No one has been able to strike terror into others and, at the same time, enjoy peace of mind. [9]
1.03 Where the fear is, happiness is not. [8]
2.01 It is better to die of hunger having lived without grief and fear, than to live with a troubled spirit, amid abundance. [6]
2.02 Any device by which one frees himself from the fear of others is a natural good. [7]
2.03 If you wish to fear nothing, consider that everything is to be feared. [8]
2.04 To see a man fearless in dangers, untainted with lusts, happy in adversity, composed in a tumult, and laughing at all those things which are generally either coveted or feared, all men must acknowledge that this can be from nothing else but a beam of divinity that influences a mortal body. [9]

3.01   It is the characteristic of a weak and diseased mind to fear the unfamiliar. [9]
3.02   True nobility is exempt from fear. [13]
3.03   There is nothing terrible in life for the man who realizes there is nothing terrible in death. [7]
3.04   The day which we fear as our last is but the birthday of eternity. [9]
4.01   Our fears are always more numerous than our dangers. [9]
4.02   A person's fears are lighter when the danger is at hand. [8]
5.01   Set aside a certain number of days, during which you shall be content with the littlest and cheapest fare, with coarse and rough dress, all the while saying to yourself: "Is this the condition that I feared?" [9]

SECTION XIII

Folly

1.01 To err is human, but to persevere in error is only the act of a fool. [13]
1.02 It is the peculiar quality of a fool to perceive the faults of others and to forget his own. [13]
1.03 Foolishness is inflicted with a hatred of itself. [8]
1.04 All fools suffer the burden of dissatisfaction with themselves. [10]
1.05 Because other people are fools, must you be so too? [10]
2.01 It is indeed pointless and foolish to seek to get from another person what one can get from oneself. [6]
2.02 Since I can get greatness of soul and nobility of mind from myself, shall I seek to get a patch of land from you, or a bit of money, or some public post? [6]
2.03 Heaven forbid! I won't overlook my own resources in such a manner. [6]
2.04 Stop honoring externals, quit turning yourself into the tool of mere matter, or of people who can supply you or deny you those material things. [6]

3.01   Then it will be in our power to understand how contemptible are the things we admire like children who regard every toy as a thing of value, who cherish necklaces bought at the price of a mere penny as dearer than their parents or their brothers. [8]

3.02   And what then, as Aristo says, is the difference between ourselves and these children, except that we elders go crazy over paintings and sculpture, and that our folly costs us dearer? [8]

3.03   There is nothing more miserable and foolish than anticipation. [9]

SECTION XIV

Freedom

1.01   Working within our sphere of control, we are naturally free, independent, and strong. [6]
1.02   Beyond that sphere, we are weak, limited, and dependent. [6]
1.03   If you pin your hopes on things outside your control, taking upon yourself things which rightfully belong to others, you are liable to stumble, fall, suffer, and blame both gods and men. [6]
1.04   But if you focus your attention only on what is truly your own concern, and leave to others what concerns them, then you will be in charge of your life. [6]
1.05   No one will be able to harm or hinder you. [6]
1.06   You will blame no one, and have no enemies. [6]
1.07   If you wish to have peace and contentment, release your attachment to all things outside your control. [6]
1.08   This is the path of freedom and happiness. [6]

1.09   If you want not just peace and contentment, but power and wealth too, you may forfeit the former in seeking the latter, and will lose your freedom and happiness along the way. [6]

2.01   Is freedom anything else than the right to live as we wish? Nothing else. [6]

2.02   Is any man free except the one who can live his life as he pleases? [2]

3.01   Freedom is not procured by a full enjoyment of what is desired, but by controlling the desire. [6]

3.02   Freedom is the greatest fruit of self-sufficiency. [7]

3.03   Freedom is not being a slave to any circumstance, to any constraint, to any chance; it means compelling fortune to enter the lists on equal terms. [8]

3.04   Freedom is the only worthy goal in life. [6]

3.05   It is won by disregarding things that lie beyond our control. [6]

3.06   Freedom, you see, is having events go in accordance with our will, never contrary to it. [6]

3.07   And the way to be free is to let go of anything that is not within your control. [6]

3.08   To freemen, threats are impotent. [13]

3.09   Only the educated are free. [6]

4.01   Freedom cannot be bought for nothing. [9]

4.02   If you hold her precious, you must hold all else of little worth. [9]

4.03   The recovery of freedom is so splendid a thing that we must not shun even death when seeking to recover it. [13]

4.04   Whoever then would be free, let him wish for nothing, let him decline nothing, which depends on others; else, he may become a slave. [6]

5.01   Freedom is participation in power. [13]

5.02 No man is free who is not master of himself. [6]
5.03 No man is free who is a slave to the flesh. [9]
5.04 A well governed appetite is the greater part of liberty. [9, 10]
6.01 Why, then, is it not possible to be free from faults? [6]
6.02 It is not possible; but this is possible: to direct your efforts incessantly to being faultless. [6]
6.03 For we must be content: by never remitting this attention, we shall escape at least a few errors. [6]
6.04 When, therefore, you see anyone eminent in honors, or power, or in high esteem on any other account, take heed not to be hurried away with the appearance, and to pronounce him happy; for if the essence of good consists of things in our own control, there will be no room for envy or emulation. [6]
7.01 But, for your part, don't wish to be a general, or a senator, or a consul, but to be free. [6]
7.02 See how many evil things you are permitting yourself to do. [6]
7.03 If it is good to use attention tomorrow, how much better is it to do so today? [6]
7.04 If tomorrow it is in your interest to attend, much more is it today, that you may be able to do so tomorrow, and may not defer it again to the third day. [6]

SECTION XV

Happiness

1.01 Tranquility and rationality are the cornerstones of happiness. [7]
1.02 There is only one way to happiness and that is to cease worrying about things which are beyond the power of our will. [6]
1.03 If you will make a man happy, do not add unto his riches but take away from his desires. [7]
2.01 Both happiness and unhappiness depend on perception. [10]
2.02 No one is ever unhappy because of someone else. [6]
2.03 The happiness of those who want to be popular depends on others; the happiness of those who seek pleasure fluctuates with moods outside their control; but the happiness of the wise grows out of their own free acts. [10]
3.01 What good is remembering past sufferings, of being unhappy now just because you were then? [9]
3.02 If you pin your hopes on things outside your control, taking upon yourself things which rightfully belong to others,

you are liable to stumble, fall, suffer, and blame both gods and men. [6]

3.03   But if you focus your attention just on what is truly your own concern, and leave to others to their own concerns then you will be the master of your own life. [6]

3.04   No one will cause you harm. No one will blame you and you will have no enemies. [6]

4.01   Humanity is fortunate because no man is unhappy, except by his own fault. [9]

4.02   A man is as unhappy as he has convinced himself. [9]

4.03   Unhappy is the man, though he rules the world, who does not consider himself supremely blessed. [8]

4.04   In order to consider himself supremely blessed, he must understand that things could be much worse but aren't! [8]

4.05   To not do that is to always be less happy than he could be. [8]

4.06   There are no greater unfortunates in the world than many of those whom people, in general, think to be happy. [8]

5.01   No man is more unhappy than he who never faces adversity. [9]

5.02   For he is not permitted to prove himself. [9]

5.03   Failing to understand the workings of one's own mind is bound to lead to unhappiness. [10]

6.01   The foundation of true joy is in one's conscience. [9]

6.02   Remember that very little is needed to make a happy life. [10]

6.03   Being happy is knowing how to be content with little. [7]

6.04   Very little is needed to make a happy life; happiness is all within yourself, in your way of thinking. [10]

6.05   Always bear this in mind that a person does not need much in life to be happy. [10]

7.01 A happy life is one which is in accordance with one's own nature. [8]
7.02 Happiness is a good flow of life. [15]
7.03 A man's true delight is to do the things he was made to do. [10]
7.04 Tranquility of mind leads to a happy life. [13]
7.05 Happiness is no other than soundness and perfection of the mind. [10]
8.01 We must meditate on what brings happiness, since when we have it, we have everything, and when we miss it, we do everything to have it. [7]
8.02 To live happily is an inward power of the soul. [10]
8.03 The happiness of your life depends upon the quality of your thoughts. [10]
8.04 No man is happy who does not think himself so. [10]
8.05 To have a happy life, guard the quality of your thoughts: take care that you entertain no notions unsuitable to virtue and reasonable nature. [10]
9.01 Your happiness depends on three things, all of which are within your power: your will, your ideas concerning the events in which you are involved, and the use you make of your ideas. [6]
9.02 Find joy in simplicity, self-respect, and indifference to what lies between virtue and vice. [10]
9.03 Love the human race. Follow the divine path. [10]
9.04 Be content to what you really are. [10]
9.05 Learn how to feel joy. [9]
9.06 Do not spoil what you have by desiring what you do not have; remember that what you now have was once among the things you only hoped for. [7]

10.01   Be moderate in order to taste the joys of life in abundance. [7]

10.02   If one oversteps the bounds of moderation, the greatest pleasures cease to please. [6]

10.03   If sensuality was happiness, then beasts were happier than men; but human felicity is lodged in the soul, not in the flesh. [8]

11.01   True happiness is to enjoy the present, without anxious dependence upon the future, not to amuse ourselves with either hopes or fears but to rest satisfied with what we have, which is sufficient, for he that is so, wants nothing. [9, 10]

11.02   The great blessings of mankind are within us and within our reach. [9, 10]

11.03   A wise man is content with his lot, whatever it may be, without wishing for what he has not. [9, 10]

SECTION XVI

Judgment

1.01 If you are pained by any external thing, it is not this thing that disturbs you, but your own judgment about it. It is in your power to erase this judgment. [10]
1.02 If anything in your own nature gives you pain, you are who hinders you from correcting your opinion. [10]
1.03 When another person harms you or speaks badly of you, remember that he acts or speaks from a supposition of being his duty. [6]
1.04 Now, it is not possible that he should follow what appears right to you, but what appears so to himself. [6]
1.05 Therefore, if he judges from a wrong appearance, he is the person who is hurt, since he too is the person who is deceived. [6]
1.06 For if anyone should suppose a true proposition to be false, the proposition is not hurt, but he who is deceived about it. [6]

1.07   Setting out, then, from these principles, you will meekly bear a person who reviles you, for you will say upon every occasion, "It seemed so to him." [6]

1.08   When you do anything from a clear judgment that it ought to be done, even though the world should make a wrong supposition about it, act right and do not be afraid of those who censure you wrongly. [6]

2.01   We are not privy to the stories behind people's actions, so we should be patient with others and suspend judgement of them, recognizing the limits of our understanding. [6]

2.02   Objective judgement, now at this very moment, unselfish action, now at this very moment, willing acceptance, now at this very moment - of all external events - that is all you need. [10]

2.03   No action will be considered blameless, unless the will was so. For by the will, the act was dictated. [8]

3.01   If you decide to do something, don't shrink from being seen doing it, even if the majority of people disapprove of it. If you are wrong to do it, then you should shrink from doing it altogether; but if you're right, then why worry how people will judge you? [6]

3.02   If you would judge, understand. [9, 10]

3.03   If you sit in judgment, investigate. If you sit in supreme power, sit in command. [8]

3.04   It is rash to condemn where you are ignorant. [9]

3.05   He, who does not wish others to be strict judges of him, cannot be strict in judging others. [13]

3.06   To become self-educated, you should condemn yourself for all those things that you criticize others. [5]

4.01   Whenever you are about to find fault with someone, ask yourself the following question: What fault of mine most nearly resembles the one I am about to criticize? [10]
4.02   The things you think about determine the quality of your mind. [10]
4.03   Your soul takes on the color of your thoughts. [10]
4.04   Treat with utmost respect your power of forming opinions, for this power alone guards you against making assumptions that are contrary to nature and judgments that overthrow the rule of reason. [10]
4.05   Do not suffer a sudden impression to overbear your judgment. [10]
4.06   Do not judge by the number, but by the weight. [13]
4.07   Watch over yourself. [9]
4.08   Be your own accuser, then your judge; ask yourself grace sometimes and, if there is need, impose upon yourself some pain. [9]
4.09   Get rid of the judgement ... get rid of the 'I am hurt' so you can get rid of the hurt itself. [10]
5.01   You always own the option of having no opinion. [10]
5.02   There is never any need to get worked up or to trouble your soul about things you cannot control. [10]
5.03   These things are not asking to be judged (by you). [10]
5.04   Leave them alone. [10]
5.05   It is within our power not to make a judgement about something, and so not disturb our minds; for nothing in itself possesses the power to form our judgements. [10]

SECTION XVII

Life/ Living

1.01   Your life is an expression of all your thoughts. [10]
1.02   When you arise in the morning, think of what a precious privilege it is to be alive - to breathe, to think, to enjoy, to love. [10]
1.03   Life is short. That is all there is to say. Get what you can from the present - thoughtfully, justly. [10]
1.04   Give yourself a gift: the present moment. [10]
1.05   Dwell on the beauty of life. Watch the stars, and see yourself running with them. [10]
2.01   Our life is what our thoughts make it. [10]
2.02   Life is neither good or evil, but only a place for good and evil. [10]
2.03   As long as you live, learn how to live. [9]
2.04   Remember that man lives only in the present, in this fleeting instant; all the rest of his life is either past and gone, or not yet revealed. [10]
3.01   If you separate from . . . everything you have done in the past, everything that disturbs you about the future . . . and

apply yourself to living the life that you are living - that is to say, the present - you can live all the time that remains to you until your death in calm, benevolence, and serenity. [10]

3.02   If you are bent on assuming a facade and never reveal yourself to anyone, in the fashion of many who live a false life that is all made up for show, it is torture to be constantly watching oneself and being fearful of being caught out of your usual role. [9]

3.03   And we are never free from concern if we think that every time anyone looks at us, he is always taking our measure; for many things happen that strip off our pretense against our will, and though all this attention to oneself is successful, yet the life of those who live under a mask cannot be happy and without anxiety. [9]

4.01   You must live for another if you wish to live for yourself. [8]

4.02   Do not live by your own rules, but in harmony with nature. [6]

4.03   Do not live life as though one had a thousand years, but live each day as the last. [10]

4.04   Do every act of your life as if it were your last. [10]

4.05   Do not spoil yourself by picturing your life as a whole. [10]

4.06   Forget the many troubles which you have encountered in the past and which you may encounter again in the future. [10]

4.07   Instead, ask yourself with regard to every present difficulty: "What is there in this situation that is unbearable and beyond endurance?" [10]

5.01   Live your life as if you are ready to say goodbye to it at any moment, as if the time left for you were some pleasant surprise. [10]

5.02   Live each day as if it is your last. [10]
5.03   Live out your life in truth and justice, tolerant of those who are neither true nor just. [10]
5.04   Adapt yourself to the life you have been given; and truly love the people with whom destiny has brought to you. [10]
6.01   Think of yourself as being dead. [10]
6.02   You have lived your life. [10]
6.03   Now, take what is left and live it properly. [10]
6.04   What doesn't transmit light creates its own darkness. [10]
7.01   A person's life is what their thoughts make it. [10]
7.02   We do not live according to reason, but according to fashion. [9]
7.03   We should conduct ourselves, not as if we ought to live for the body but, as if we could not live without it. [9]
7.04   While you live, while it is in your power, be good. [10]
7.05   Live for your neighbor if you would live for yourself. [9]
8.01   Your days are numbered. [10]
8.02   Use them to throw open the windows of your soul to the sun. [10]
8.03   If you do not, the sun will soon set, and you with it. [10]
8.04   No one loses any other life than the one he now lives, nor does one live any other life than that which he will lose. [10]
9.01   Long life is denied us; therefore, let us do something to show that we have lived. [13]
9.02   Some men spend their whole life furnishing for themselves the things proper to life without realizing that at our birth each of us was poured a mortal brew to drink. [7]
9.03   Some things are in our control and others not. [6]

9.04   Things in our control are opinion, pursuit, desire, aversion, and, in other words, whatever are our own actions. [6]
9.05   Things not in our control are body, property, reputation, command, and, in other words, whatever are not our own actions. [6]
9.06   The point is not how long you live, but how nobly you live. [9]
10.01   Whoever values peace of mind and the health of the soul will live the best of all possible lives. [10]
10.02   Today, when the crisis calls you, will you go off and display your recitation and harp on, "How cleverly I compose dialogues"? [9]
10.03   Nay, fellow men. Make this your object, "Look how I failed what I willed not to get." [9]
10.04   Look how I escaped what I willed to avoid. [9]
10.05   Let death come and you shall know; bring me pains, prison, dishonor, condemnation. [9]
10.06   It takes a whole of life to learn how to live, and - even more surprising - it takes a whole of life to learn how to die. [9]
10.07   The art of living well and the art of dying well are one. [7]
11.01   You want to live, but do you know how to live? [9]
11.02   You are scared of dying. Then tell me, is the kind of life you lead really any different from being dead? [9]
11.03   He, who does not know how to die well, will live poorly. [9]
11.04   No man enjoys the true taste of life but he who is ready and willing to quit it. [9]
12.01   This life is only a prelude to eternity. [9]

12.02   External things are not the problem. [10]
12.03   It is your assessment of them that is the problem, which you can erase right now. [10]
12.04   Imagine if you were now dead, or had not lived before his moment. [10]
12.05   Now view the rest of your life as a bonus. [10]
12.06   Every man's life lies within the present; for the past is spent and done with, and the future is uncertain. [10]
12.07   Discard everything except these few truths: we can live only in the present moment, in this brief now; all the rest of our life is dead and buried or shrouded in uncertainty. [10]
13.01   Short is the life we lead, and small our patch of earth. [10]
13.02   Tomorrow is nothing, today is too late; the good lived yesterday. [10]
13.03   For a man can lose neither the past nor the future; for how can one take from him that which is not his? [10]
13.04   So remember these two points: first, that each thing is of like form from everlasting and comes around again in its cycle, and that it signifies not whether a man shall look upon the same things for a hundred years or two hundred, or for an infinity of time; second, that the longest lived and the shortest lived man, when they come to die, lose one and the same thing. [10]

SECTION XVIII

Misfortune

1.01   To bear misfortune in a noble manner is a good fortune. [10]
1.02   Happy is the man who can endure the highest and the lowest fortune. [8]
1.03   He, who has endured such vicissitudes with equanimity, has deprived misfortune of its power. [8]
2.01   To blame others for one's own misfortune is a sign of want of education. [6]
2.02   To blame oneself of one's misfortune shows that one's education has begun. [6]
2.03   To blame neither oneself nor others for one's misfortune shows that one's education is complete. [6]
2.04   If you must be affected by other people's misfortunes, show them pity instead of contempt. [6]
2.05   Drop this readiness to hate and take offence. [6]
3.01   But if someone is wretched and cowardly, what on earth can one do for him except write letters for him as though on behalf of a corpse, "Do please grant us the corpse of this man

and a pint of his miserable blood"; for in truth such a person is merely a corpse and a pint of blood, and nothing more. [6]
3.02   If he amounted to anything more, he would realize that no one suffers misfortune because of the actions of another. [6]
4.01   Misfortune is the test of a person's merit. [9]
4.02   Not to feel one's misfortune is not human, not to bear them is not manly. [9]
5.01   Nothing is more wretched or foolish than to anticipate misfortunes. [9, 10]
5.02   What madness is it to be expecting evil before it comes. [9, 10]

SECTION XIX

Peace

1.01 The name of peace is sweet, and the thing itself is beneficial, but there is a great difference between peace and servitude. [13]
1.02 Peace is freedom in tranquility; servitude is the worst of all evils, to be resisted not only by war, but even by death. [13]
1.03 Tranquility is a certain quality of mind, which no condition or fortune can either exalt or depress. [9]
2.01 It isn't death, pain, exile or anything else that accounts for the way we act but our opinion about death, pain and the rest. [6]
2.02 Only the just man enjoys peace of mind. [7]
2.03 The first rule is to keep an untroubled spirit. [10]
2.04 The second is to look things in the face and know them for what they are. [10]
2.05 He who lives in harmony with himself lives in harmony with the universe. [10]
3.01 Men are disturbed not by things, but by the views which they take of things. [6]

3.02   Thus, death is nothing terrible; else, it would have appeared so to Socrates. [6]

3.03   But the terror consists in our notion of death; that it is terrible. [6]

3.04   Therefore, when we are hindered, or disturbed, or grieved, let us never attribute it to others, but to ourselves; that is, to our own views. [6]

3.05   It is the action of an uneducated person to reproach others for his own misfortunes; of one starting his education, to reproach himself; and of one perfectly educated, to reproach neither others nor himself. [6]

SECTION XX

Righteousness

1.01 Do not seek the good in external things; seek it within you. [6]
1.02 If you desire to be good, begin by believing that you are wicked. [6]
1.03 The largest part of goodness is the will to become good. [9]
1.04 Let goodness go with the doing. [10]
1.05 There is sufficient reward in the mere consciousness of a good action. [13]
1.06 Know the joy of life by piling good deed on good deed until no rift or cranny appears between them. [10]
1.07 The best way to keep good acts in memory is to refresh them with new. [12]
2.01 He who is running a race ought to endeavor and strive to the utmost of his ability to come off victorious; but it is utterly wrong for him to trip up his competitor, or to push him aside. [3]

2.02   So in life, it is not unfair for one to seek for oneself what may be beneficial; but it is not right to take it from another. [3]

2.03   To refrain from imitation is the best revenge. [10]

3.01   Waste no more time arguing what a good man should be. Be one. [10]

3.02   Waste no more time talking about great souls and how they should be, become one yourself! [10]

3.03   Death hangs over you. [10]

3.04   While you still live, while you can, do good. [10]

4.01   Whatever moral rules you have deliberately proposed to yourself, abide by them as if they were laws and as if you may be guilty of impiety by violating any of them. [6]

4.02   Don't regard what anyone says of you; for this is no concern of yours after all. [6]

SECTION XXI

Self-Discipline/ Self-Control

1.01   Most powerful is he who has the ability to rule his own self. [8]
1.02   Man conquers the world by conquering himself. [15]
1.03   The worst ruler is one who cannot rule himself. [11]
1.04   If you are ruled by your mind, you are a king; if by your body, you are a slave. [11]
1.05   When force of circumstance upsets your composure, lose no time in recovering your self-control, and do not remain out of tune longer than you can help. [10]
1.06   Habitual return to harmony will increase your mastery of it. [10]
2.01   It is easier to exclude harmful passions than to rule them, and to deny them admittance than to control them after they have been admitted. [9]
2.02   You have power over your mind - not outside events. [10]
2.03   Realize this, and you will find strength. [10]

2.04   Those who are well constituted in the body endure both heat and cold: and so those who are well constituted in the soul endure both anger and grief, and excessive joy and the other affects. [6]
3.01   Be tolerant with others and strict with yourself. [10]
3.02   Stick to what is in front of you - idea, action, utterance. [10]
3.03   Do not be careless in deeds. Do not be confused in words. Do not be rambling in thought. [10]
3.04   Let no act be done without a purpose. [10]
3.05   Whatever you do, do it with all your might. [13]
3.06   Work, therefore, to be able to say to every harsh appearance, "You are but an appearance and not absolutely the thing you appear to be." [6]
3.07   And then examine it by those rules which you have; first and chiefly, by this: whether it concerns the things which are in our own control, or those which are not; and, if it concerns anything not in our control, be prepared to say that it is nothing to you. [6]
4.01   Confine yourself to the present. [10]
4.02   Each day provides its own gifts. [10]
4.03   Past and future have no power over you - just the present - and even that can be minimized. [10]
4.04   Do not waste what remains of your life in speculating about your neighbors, unless with a view to some mutual benefit. [10]
4.05   To wonder what so-and-so is doing and why, or what he is saying, or thinking, or scheming - in other words, anything that distracts you - means a loss of opportunity for some other tasks. [10]

5.01   Whatever rules you have adopted, abide by them as laws, and as if you would be a sin to violate them; and do not regard what anyone says of you, for this is none of your concern. [6]

5.02   How long, then, will you delay your noblest improvements? [6]

5.03   You have received the philosophic principles with which you ought to be conversant; and you have been conversant with them. [6]

5.04   What excuse do you have for this delay in self-reformation? [6]

5.05   You are no longer a boy but a grown man. [6]

5.06   If, therefore, you will be negligent and slothful, and always add procrastination to procrastination, purpose to purpose, and day after day you attend only to yourself, you will insensibly continue to accomplish nothing and, living and dying, remain of vulgar mind. [6]

5.07   This instant, then, think yourself worthy of living as a grown up man. [6]

5.08   Let whatever appears to be the best, be to you an unbreakable law. [6]

5.09   And if any instance of pain or pleasure, glory or disgrace be set before you, remember that now is the battle, now is the Olympiad, it cannot be put off, and by one failure and defeat, honor may be lost or - won. [6]

5.10   Thus, Socrates became perfect, improving himself on everything and following reason alone. [6]

5.11   And though you are not yet a Socrates, you ought to live as one seeking to be a Socrates. [6]

SECTION XXII

Self-Improvement

1.01   Know yourself; this is the major goal. [9]
1.02   Know first who you are, and then adorn yourself accordingly. [6]
1.03   Say to yourself what you would be; and then do what you have to do. [6]
1.04   One who desires to excel should endeavor in those areas that are most excellent. [6]
1.05   Get into the habit of asking yourself in relation to any action taken by another: "What is his point of reference here?" [10]
1.06   But begin with yourself: examine yourself first. [10]
2.01   If you aim to improve, be content to be thought of as foolish and dull with regard to externals. [6]
2.02   Do not desire to be thought of as one who knows everything; and though you should appear to others as a person of importance, distrust yourself. [6]
2.03   Be assured that it is not easy to keep your will in harmony with nature and to secure externals; but while you are

immersed in one, you must, out of necessity, neglect the other. [6]

3.01   To things which you bear with impatience, you should accustom yourself, and by habit, you will bear them well. [9]

3.02   Virtue is a habit of the mind, consistent with nature, moderation and reason. [13]

4.01   Great is the power of habit. [13]

4.02   It teaches us to bear fatigue and to despise wounds and pain. [13]

4.03   Vicious habits are so great a stain to human nature, and so detestable in themselves, that every person with right mind would avoid them, even though they would be always be concealed both from God and man, and entails no future punishment. [13]

5.01   Every night, we should ask ourselves: What infirmity have I mastered today? [8]

5.02   What passions opposed? [8]

5.03   What temptations resisted? [8]

5.04   What virtues acquired? [8]

5.05   Every habit and faculty are confirmed and strengthened by the corresponding actions, that of walking by walking, that of running by running. [6]

5.06   If you wish to be a good reader, read; if you wish to be a good writer, write. [6]

5.07   If you should give up reading for thirty days, and be engaged in something else, you will know what happens. [6]

5.08   Also, if you lie in bed for ten days, get up and try to take a rather long walk, you will see how wobbly your legs are. [6]

5.09   In general, therefore, if you want to do something, make a habit of it. [6]

5.10   If you do not want to do something, refrain from doing it, and accustom yourself to doing something else instead. [6]
6.01   For heaven's sake, do simple, little things, and then proceed to bigger things. [6]
7.01   When you find yourself reluctant to rise early in the morning, make this short speech to yourself: I am getting up now to do the business of a man. [10]
7.02   Am I out of humor for going about what I was made for, and for the sake of which I was sent into the world? [10]
7.03   Was I then designed for nothing but to doze and keep warm beneath the counterpane? [10]
7.04   Well! But this is a comfortable way of living. [10]
8.01   Tranquility is nothing else than the good organization of the mind. [10]
8.02   Do a self-discovery. [2]
8.03   The time when most of you should withdraw to be with and just yourselves is when you are forced to be in a crowd. [7]
8.04   Withdraw deep within your soul, find peace and renew yourself. [10]

SECTION XXIII

Speech

1.01 The most beautiful thing in the world is freedom of speech. [5]
1.02 Speech is the gift of all, but the thought of few. [11]
1.03 Thought is the fountain of speech. [3]
1.04 Speech is the index of the mind. [9]
1.05 Men's language is as their lives. [9]
1.06 All has the gift of speech, but few possess wisdom in their speeches. [12]
1.07 Consider in silence what anyone says: speech both conceals and reveals the inner soul of man. [12]
2.01 Let us say what we feel, and feel what we say; let speech harmonize with life. [9]
2.02 Conversation has a kind of charm about it, an insinuating and insidious something that elicits secrets just like love or liquor. [8]
2.03 It is a great thing to know the season for speech and the season for silence. [8]

2.04 It is easy to distinguish between the joking that reflects good breeding and that which is coarse - the first type of joking, if aired at an appropriate moment of mental relaxation, is becoming in the most serious of men, whereas the second type of joking is unworthy of any free person if the content is indecent or the expression is obscene. [13]
3.01 People who talk well but do nothing are like musical instruments; the sound is all they have to offer. [5]
3.02 First, learn the meaning of what you say, and then speak. [6]
3.03 Grasp the subject; the words will follow. [11]
3.04 In conversations, avoid the extremes of forwardness and being too reserved. [12]
3.05 Brevity is a great charm of eloquence. [13]
3.06 Speech devoted to truth should be straightforward and plain. [9]
4.01 Silence is one of the great arts of conversation. [13]
4.02 Keep silence for the most part, and speak only when you must; speak briefly. [6]
4.03 Silence is safer than speech. [6]
4.04 The first virtue is to restrain the tongue; he who knows how to be silent, even though he is in the right, has virtue that approaches that of gods. [11]
4.05 The primary virtue is: hold your tongue; he who knows how to keep quiet is close to God. [12]
4.06 Consider it the greatest of all virtues to restrain the tongue. [12]
4.07 The first wisdom is to restrain the tongue. [12]
4.08 Speak briefly and to the point. [12]
5.01 Better to trip with the feet than with the tongue. [15]

5.02   What view is one likely to take of the state of a person's mind when his speech is wild and incoherent and knows no constraint? [9]

5.03   Whenever the speech is corrupted, so is the mind. [8]

5.04   We cannot control the evil tongues of others; but a good life enables us to disregard them. [11]

6.01   Though laughter is allowed, a horse-laugh is abominable. [13]

6.02   It is the same to remove the aroma from wormwood as it is to remove the outspokenness from speech? [1]

7.01   Discourse on virtue and they pass by in droves. [5]

7.02   Whistle and dance the shimmy, and you've got an audience. [5]

8.01   Every man's nature is concealed with many folds of disguise, and covered as it were with various veils. [13]

8.02   His brows, his eyes, and very often his countenance, are deceitful, and his speech is most commonly a lie. [13]

8.03   Sometimes, direct quarrel springs from the lightest words. [11]

SECTION XXIV

Thinking

1.01 All is as thinking makes it so. [10]
1.02 Everything is but what we think it. [10]
1.03 Everything hangs on one's thinking. [9]
1.04 Our lives are what our thoughts make them. [10]
1.05 Your mind will be like its habitual thoughts; for the soul becomes dyed with the color of its thoughts. Soak it then in such trains of thoughts as, for example: Where life is possible at all, a right life is possible. [10]
1.06 Unblessed is he who thinks himself unblessed. [9]
2.01 Imagine for yourself a character, a model personality, whose example you are determined to follow in private as well as in public. [6]
2.02 Deliberate much before saying or doing anything, for you will not have the power of recalling what is said or done. [6]
2.03 Do not dress your thoughts in too fine a raiment. And do not be a man of superfluous words or superfluous deeds. [10]

2.04 One original thought is worth a thousand mindless quotes. [5]
3.01 Do every act of your life as if it were your last. [10]
3.02 In other words, your life is short. [10]
3.03 You must make the most of the present with the aid of reason and justice. Since it is possible that you may be quitting life at this very moment, govern every act and thought accordingly. [10]
3.04 The mind is a master over every kind of fortune; the mind acts in both ways; it can cause happiness and it can cause misery. [9]
3.05 Happiness and freedom begin with a clear understanding of one principle: Some things are within our control, and some things are not. [6]
4.01 There are two things that must be rooted out in human beings - arrogant opinion and mistrust. [6]
4.02 Arrogant opinion expects that there is nothing further needed, and mistrust assumes that under the torrent of circumstance, there can be no happiness. [6]
4.03 Change your attitude to the things that bother you and you will be more mindful of them. [10]
4.04 But it sometimes comes about that, when we have properly granted certain premises, certain conclusions are derived from them that, though false, nonetheless follow from them. [6]
4.05 What am I to do, then? Accept the false conclusion? And how is that possible? [6]
4.06 Then should I say that I was wrong to accept the premises? [6]
4.07 No, this isn't permissible either. Or say: That doesn't follow from the premises? But that again isn't permissible. [6]

4.08   So, what is one to do in such circumstances? [6]
4.09   Isn't it the same as with debts? [6]
4.10   Just as having borrowed on some occasion isn't enough to make somebody a debtor, but it is necessary in addition that he continues to owe the money and hasn't paid off the loan; likewise, our having accepted the premises isn't enough to make it necessary for us to accept the inference, but we have to continue to accept the premises. [6]
5.01   Yet if we place the choice in good, the preservation of our relationships itself becomes a good. [6]
5.02   And besides, he who gives up certain external things achieves the good through that. For example, "My father is depriving me of money." [6]
5.03   But he isn't causing you any harm. [6]
5.04   Another example, "My brother is going to get the greater share of the land." [6]
5.05   Let him have as much as he wishes. [6]
5.06   He won't be getting any of your decency, will he, or of your loyalty, or of your brotherly love? [6]
5.07   For who can disinherit you of possessions such as those? [6]

SECTION XXV

Time

1.01   Time is a sort of river of passing events, and strong is its current; no sooner is a thing brought to sight than it is swept by and another takes its place, and this too will be swept away. [10]
1.02   The swiftness of time is infinite, as is still more evident when we look back on the past. [9]
2.01   Time is the one thing that is given to everyone in equal measure. [9]
2.02   Your time has a limit set to it. [10]
2.03   Use it, then, to advance your enlightenment; or it will be gone and will never be in your power again. [10]
2.04   Limit time to the present. [10]
2.05   Meditate upon your last hour. [10]
3.01   Nothing is ours except time. [9]
3.02   Everyone has time if he likes. People are often busy and stick to it out of their own free will. They think that to be busy is a proof of happiness. [9]

3.03   It is not that we have so little time but that we lose so much ... . [9]

3.04   The life we receive is not short but we make it so; we are not ill provided but we use what we have wastefully. [9]

4.01   The greatest loss of time is delay and expectation, which depend upon the future. [8]

4.02   We let go the present, which we have in our power, and look forward to that which depends upon chance, and so relinquish a certainty for an uncertainty. [8]

4.03   We all sorely complain of the shortness of time, and yet we have much more than we know what to do with. [8]

4.04   Our lives are either spent in doing nothing at all, or in doing nothing with purpose, or in doing nothing that we ought to do. [8]

4.05   We are always complaining that our days are few, and yet acting as though there would be no end of them. [8]

5.01   How much time can a man save if he does not pay attention to what his neighbor says or does or thinks? [10]

5.02   Time is the most valuable thing that a man can spend. [5]

5.03   A man who has taken your time recognizes no debt; yet, it is the one he can never repay. [9]

SECTION XXVI

Truth

1.01   Truths are open to everyone, and the claims aren't all staked yet. [9]
1.02   We know nothing really; for truth lies deep down. [5]
1.03   By nature, our minds possess an insatiable desire to know the truth. [13]
2.01   The language of truth is unvarnished enough. [9]
2.02   Simple is the language of truth. [9]
2.03   The expression of truth is simplicity. [9]
3.01   If you seek truth, you will not seek victory by dishonorable means, and if you find truth, you will become invincible. [6]
3.02   Everything we hear is an opinion, not a fact. Everything we see is a perspective, not the truth. [10]
3.03   No one was ever injured by the truth, but he who persists in self-deception and ignorance. [10]
4.01   Through doubt, we arrive at the truth. [13]
4.02   Time discovered truth. [8]
4.03   Time is the herald of truth. [13]

SECTION XXVII

Vanity

1.01   Boasting, like gilded armor, is very different inside - compared to outside. [5]

1.02   Those who boast of their lineage, brag on what they owe to others. [8]

1.03   It is not only arrogant, but also shameless, for a man to disregard the world's opinion of himself. [13]

1.04   After all, what does everlasting fame mean? Mere vanity. [10]

2.01   It is a disgrace to let ignorance and vanity do more with us than prudence and principle. [10]

2.02   It is only luxury and avarice that make poverty grievous to us; for it is a very small matter that does our business, and when we are provided against cold, hunger, and thirst, all the rest is but vanity and excess. [9]

3.01   In prosperity, let us most carefully avoid pride, disdain, and arrogance. [13]

3.02   That which is given with pride and ostentation is an ambition rather than a bounty. [8]

SECTION XXVIII

Virtue

1.01   Virtue is the health of the soul. [1]
1.02   Virtue is never denied from anyone; she is open to all, accepts all, invites all - gentlemen, freemen, slaves, kings, and exiles; she selects neither house nor fortune; she is satisfied with a human being without adjuncts. [9]
2.01   Virtue is its own reward. [13]
2.02   Honor is the reward of virtue. [13]
2.03   Virtue is that perfect good, which is the complement of a happy life; the only immortal thing that belongs to mortality. [9]
2.04   While all other things are uncertain, evanescent, and ephemeral, virtue alone is fixed with deep roots; it can neither be overthrown by any violence nor moved from its place. [13]
2.05   Virtue is uniform, conformable to reason, and of unvarying consistency; nothing can be added to it that can make it more than virtue; nothing can be taken from it. [13]
3.01   Patience is the greatest of all virtues. [11]

3.02   A thankful heart is not only the greatest virtue but the parent of all the other virtues. [13]
3.03   A thankful heart is the greatest virtue. [13]
3.04   Gratitude is a virtue that is commonly complemented by reward. [7]
3.05   Whatever is graceful is virtuous, and whatever is virtuous is graceful. [13]
4.01   The existence of virtue depends entirely upon its use. [13]
4.02   Nature does not bestow virtue; to be good is an art. [9]
4.03   The whole glory of virtue resides in the endeavor. [13]
4.04   Virtue depends partly upon training and partly upon practice; you must learn first, and then strengthen your learning by actions. [9]
4.05   It is not enough merely to possess virtue, as if it were an art; it should be practiced. [13]
4.06   Those who have virtue always in their lips, and neglect it in their practice, are like a harp, which emits a sound pleasing to others, while itself is insensible to the music. [5]
5.01   Remove severe restraint and what will become of virtue? [8]
5.02   Virtue consists of three parts, - temperance, fortitude, and justice. [7]
5.03   Virtue cannot dwell with wealth either in a city or in a house. [5]
5.04   Living virtuously is equal to living in accordance with one's experience of the actual course of nature. [3]
5.05   The more virtuous a man is, the less easily he suspects others to be vicious. [13]
5.06   Modesty is the color of virtue. [5]
6.01   Calamity is virtue's opportunity. [8]

6.02   Poverty is a virtue which one can teach oneself. [5]

6.03   We are born to lose and to perish, to hope and to fear, to displease ourselves and others; and there is no antidote against a common calamity but virtue; for the foundation of true joy is in the conscience. [9]

7.01   Few are those who wish to be endowed with virtue. [13]

7.02   It is difficult to persuade mankind that the love of virtue is the love of oneself. [13]

7.03   Virtue depends partly upon education and partly upon practice; first, you must learn; and then strengthen your learning by doing. [9]

7.04   If this be true, not only do the doctrines of wisdom help us but the precepts also, which check and banish our emotions by a sort of official decree. [9]

8.01   If virtue promises happiness, prosperity and peace, then progress in virtue is progress in each of these, for to whatever point the perfection of anything brings us, progress is always an approach toward it. [6]

8.02   Consider who it is that you praise when you praise people dispassionately: is it those who are just or unjust? - 'Those who are just.' - The temperate or the intemperate? - 'The temperate.' - The self-controlled or the dissolute? - 'The self-controlled.' - You should know, then, that if you make yourself a person of that kind, you'll be making yourself beautiful; but if you neglect these virtues, you are bound to be ugly, whatever techniques you adopt to make yourself appear beautiful. [6]

SECTION XXIX

Wealth/ Riches

1.01 He who needs riches the least, enjoys riches the most. [7]
1.02 Wealth does not consist in having great possessions, but in having few wants. [6]
1.03 To be content with what we possess is the greatest and most secure of riches. [13]
1.04 A person's worth is measured by the worth of what he values. [10]
1.05 Self-sufficiency is the greatest of all wealth. [7]
1.06 Whoever does not regard what he has as most ample wealth is unhappy, though he may be the master of the world. [6]
2.01 What is the proper limit for wealth? [8]
2.02 It is, first, to have what is necessary; and, second, to have what is enough. [8]
2.03 For many men, the acquisition of riches has been, not an end but, a beginning of troubles. [7]
2.04 A great estate is a great disadvantage to those who do not know how to use it, for nothing is more common than to

see wealthy persons live scandalously and miserably; riches do not bring them closer to virtue and happiness; therefore, it is precept and principle, not an estate, which make a man good for something. [10]

3.01   Riches are a cause of evil, not because of themselves, as they do no evil, but because they goad men on to evil. [14]

3.02   A great fortune is a great slavery. [8]

3.03   To many, the acquisition of riches has not been an end to their miseries, but a change in their fortunes or misfortunes. The fault is not in the riches, but in their dispositions. [8]

3.04   Riches do not exhilarate us so much with their possession, as they torment us with their loss. [7]

3.05   The things that men admire and work so hard to get prove useless to them once these things are theirs. [6]

4.01   Just as great and princely wealth is squandered in a moment when it comes into the hands of a bad owner, limited wealth increases by proper use if it is entrusted to a good guardian. [9]

4.02   It is the sign of a weak mind to be unable to bear wealth. [9]

4.03   As with men who drink wine, and some of them get delirious while others morose, so is with gaining wealth. [1]

5.01   If you live according to the dictates of nature, you will never be poor; if according to the notions of man, you will never be rich. [8]

5.02   Live according to your income. [2]

5.03   Do not buy what you want, but what you have need of. [11]

6.01   Think of what you have, rather than what you lack. [10]

6.02   Of the things you have, select the best and then reflect how eagerly you would have sought them if you did not have them. [10]

6.03   The only wealth which you will keep forever is the wealth you have given away. [10]

6.04   Remember, not one penny can we take with us into the unknown land. [9]

SECTION XXX

Wisdom

1.01 Wisdom does not show itself so much in precept as in life - in firmness of mind and a mastery of appetite. [9, 10]
1.02 Wisdom teaches us to do as well as we talk; and to make our words and actions all of a color. [9, 10]
1.03 The best sign of wisdom is the consistency between the words and deeds. [9]
2.01 Wisdom is not only to be acquired, but also to be enjoyed. [13]
2.02 It is not enough to acquire wisdom; it is also necessary to utilize it. [13]
2.03 It is impossible to live a pleasant life without living wisely and well and justly. [7]
2.04 And it is impossible to live wisely and well and justly without living a pleasant life. [7]
2.05 We cannot live pleasantly without living wisely and nobly and righteously. [7]
2.06 No one can lead a happy life, or even one that is bearable, without the pursuit of wisdom. The perfection of

wisdom is what makes life happy, although even the beginnings of wisdom make life bearable. [9]

2.07   Yet this conviction, clear as it is, needs to be strengthened and given deeper roots through daily reflection; making noble resolutions is not as important as keeping the resolutions you have already made. [9]

3.01   Wisdom is the only thing which can relieve us from the passions and the fear of danger, and which can teach us to bear the injuries of fortune itself with moderation, and which shows us all the ways which lead to tranquility and peace. [13]

3.02   Prosperity demands of us more prudence and moderation than adversity. [13]

3.03   Adversity increases our wisdom; prosperity destroys our appreciation of righteousness. [9]

3.04   Man must suffer to be wise. [13]

4.01   Appearances to the mind are of four kinds. [6]

4.02   Things either are what they appear to be; or they neither are, nor appear to be; or they are, and do not appear to be; or they are not, and yet appear to be. [6]

4.03   To judge appropriately in all these cases is the wise man's task. [6]

4.04   The wise man will always reflect concerning the quality, not the quantity, of life. [9]

4.05   There is nothing the wise man does reluctantly. [9]

5.01   Wise leaders generally have wise counselors because it takes wise persons themselves to distinguish and employ wise assistants. [5]

5.02   It takes a wise man to discover a wise man. [5]

6.01   The wise man sees in the misfortune of others what he should avoid. [10]

6.02   The wise man knows nothing if he cannot benefit from his wisdom. [13]
6.03   One needs to apply wisdom and not just acquire it. [13]
6.04   The wise person knows that it is futile to project hopes and fears on the future. [6]
6.05   This only leads to forming melodramatic representations in your mind and wasting time. [6]
7.01   To be wise is the most desirable thing in the world. [13]
7.02   Many persons might have achieved wisdom had they not supposed that they already possessed it. [9]
7.03   He, who seeks wisdom, is a wise man; he, who thinks he has found it, is mad. [9]
7.04   It is sometimes the pinnacle of wisdom to fake stupidity. [11]
7.05   The two powers which … constitute a wise man are those of bearing and forbearing. [6]
8.01   He is a wise man who does not grieve for the things which he has not, but rejoices for those which he has. [6]
8.02   He who uses wisdom, utilizes the knowledge which is about God. [6]
8.03   The wise man meddles little or not at all in other people's affairs and does his own things. [3]
9.01   Do not be wise in words - be wise in deeds. [10]
9.02   Do not try to pretend being wise. [6]
9.03   If you want to live a wise life, live it on your own terms and in your own eyes. [6]
9.04   Look deep into the hearts of men, and see what delights and disgusts the wise. [10]
9.05. If you don't know, ask. [9]
9.06   You will be a fool for the moment, but a wise man for the rest of your life. [9]

SECTION XXXI

Wisdom And Folly

1.01 There is only a finger's difference between a wise man and a fool. [5]
1.02 Wise men are more dependent on fools than fools on wise men. [12]
1.03 A clever person learns more from fools than fools learn from the wise. [11]
1.04 Wise men profit more from fools than fools from wise men; for the wise men shun the mistakes of fools, but fools do not imitate the successes of the wise. [11]
1.05 The wise are instructed by reason, average minds by experience, the stupid by necessity, and the brute by instinct. [13]
2.01 It is the nature of the wise to resist pleasures, but the foolish is a slave to them. [6]
2.02 Wise people are in want of nothing, and yet need many things. [3]

2.03   On the other hand, nothing is needed by fools, for they do not understand how to use anything, but are in want of everything. [3]

2.04   If others are wise, do not quarrel with them; if others are fools, ignore them. [6]

3.01   The misfortune of the wise is better than the prosperity of the fool. [7]

3.02   Time relieves the foolish of sorrow, but reason relieves the wise. [6]

4.01   To the wise, life is a challenge; to the fool, a solution. [10]

4.02   The wise man neither rejects life nor fears death... just as he does not necessarily choose the largest amount of food, but, rather, the pleasantest food, so he prefers not the longest time, but the most pleasant. [7]

SECTION XXXII

Wrongs/ Mistakes

1.01   Whosoever does wrong, wrongs himself; whosoever does injustice, does it to himself, making himself evil. [10]
1.02   He, who will not pardon others, must not himself expect to be pardoned. [9]
1.03   Not to commit wrong leads one towards peace of mind. [9]
2.01   A wrongdoer is often a man who has left something undone, not always one who has done something. [10]
2.02   The sinner sins against himself; the wrongdoer wrongs himself, becoming the worse by his own action. [10]
2.03   It is better to do wrong rarely and to own it, and to act right for the most part, than to admit rarely that you have done wrong, yet do wrong often. [6]
3.01   An awareness of your own wrongdoing is the first step to salvation...you have to catch yourself doing it before you can correct it. [9]
3.02   It is silly to try to escape other people's faults. [10]
3.03   They are inescapable. [10]

3.04   Just try to escape your own. [10]
4.01   It is a proof of nobility of mind to despise injuries. [9]
4.02   Any man can make mistakes, but only an idiot persists in committing them. [13]
4.03   Leave other people's mistakes where they lie. [10]
4.04   The offender needs pity, not wrath; those who need to be corrected should be treated with tact and gentleness; and one must be always ready to learn from the situation. [10]
5.01   Forgiveness is better than revenge, for forgiveness is the sign of a gentle nature, but revenge is the sign of a savage nature. [6]
5.02   Leave the wrong done by another where the wrong arose. [10]
5.03   It is often better not to see an insult than to avenge it. [9]
5.04   The best revenge is not to be like your enemy. [10]
5.05   Reject your sense of injury, and the injury itself disappears. [10]
5.06   The best revenge is to be unlike him who performed the injury. [10]

APPENDIX:
The Stoic Philosophers

[1] Aristo of Chios [Aristo] (c. 310 - c. 240 B.C.)

[2] Aulus Persius Flaccus [Persius] (34 - 62 A.D.)

[3] Chrysippus (of Soli) [Chrysippus] (c. 280 - c. 206 B.C.)

[4] Cleanthes (of Assos) [Cleanthes] (331 - 232 B.C.)

[5] Diogenes of Babylon [Diogenes] (c. 230 - c. 150 B.C.)

[6] Epictetus (of Hierapolis) [Epictetus] (c. 55 - c. 135 A.D.)

[7] Epicurus (341 - 270 B.C.)

[8] Lucius Annaeus Seneca [Seneca the Elder] (c. 54 B.C. - c. 39 A.D.)

[9] Lucius Annaeus Seneca [Seneca the Younger] (c. 4 B.C. - 65 A.D.)

[10] Marcus Aurelius [Marcus] (121 - 180 A.D.)

[11] Marcus Porcius Cato [Cato the Elder; Cato the Censor] (234 - 248 B.C.)

[12] Marcus Porcius Cato [Cato the Younger] (95 - 46 B.C.)

[13] Marcus Tullius Cicero [Cicero] (106 - 43 B.C.)

[14] Posidonius (of Apamea) (c. 135 - 51 B.C.)

[15] Zeno (of Citium) [Zeno] (c. 334 - 262 B.C.)

ABOUT THE AUTHORS

James L. Jordan, PhD, PhD, and Deovina N. Jordan, PhD, MD, celebrate more than 80 years of combined remarkable experiences in their professional lives. They are noted for their significant achievements and outstanding successes in science, management, healthcare, and higher education (with senior professorial ranks). Dr. James L. Jordan and Dr. Deovina N. Jordan have authored several books and many peer reviewed journal articles. They are developing scientific theories. Dr. James L. Jordan and Dr. Deovina N. Jordan have been highlighted in over 20 editions of Marquis Who's Who (in America, West, World, Education, Medicine, Healthcare, and Worldwide Lifetime Achievement).

Dr. James L. Jordan and Dr. Deovina N. Jordan live in a farm in the mountains with their two Yorkshire terriers and abundant wildlife. They share a love for wisdom literature and nature.

ABOUT THE BOOK

This book contains the teachings/ sayings/ statements of 15 Stoic philosophers who taught people two thousand years ago how to appreciate their loved ones and other people in their lives. These philosophers taught people to live life to the fullest and be happy with what they have. The Stoics, as they are referred to, recognized that material goods do not bring happiness. Instead, according to them, a creative mind is more attuned with true wealth. They also taught people to be ethical and not just preach about ethics.

Stoicism was an ancient Greek school of philosophy founded in Athens by Zeno of Citium in the early 3rd century B.C.. This school of philosophy has influenced religion. Before the Christian era, the converts of Judaism knew more about Stoicism than the teachings of Moses. Rabbis, who wrote the Talmud, presented themselves as Stoics. The early Christians, who emerged from a world with Judaism, were very familiar with Stoic teachings. The Apostle Paul, who gave respect to Jewish and Greek ideas during the formation of the early Christian church, may have been influenced by the

Stoic philosophy. The influence of Stoicism lasted through the modern times since it left its mark during the early formation of Christianity.

In addition, Stoicism has had a major impact on humankind. It has been linked to greater calmness, particularly with regard to things and events beyond one's control and, as a consequence, to happiness. By knowing what is in one's power to control, one can lead a more productive life and, consequently, a more meaningful and happy life. Also, by differentiating what one can control versus what one cannot, one can be more focused in life, permitting one to do the greatest good during one's lifetime. Moreover, by knowing how to minimize negative emotions, one can maximize one's gratitude and joy in life.

This book is a tribute to the Stoic philosophers. It focuses on what they actually said (their teachings, sayings, statements). The names of the 15 Stoic philosophers are provided in the appendix. The teachings/ sayings/ statements are followed by numbers in brackets to identify the source. The topics are arranged alphabetically.

Finally, this is a book without commentary by the authors. As such, the authors made no attempt to modify what the Stoics said. That kind of commentary is left to the reader who can then use the teachings/ sayings/ statements in the book for his/ her own benefit and self-discovery.

BOOKS AND ARTICLES WRITTEN BY THE AUTHORS

God: Answering the Mysteries of God, God's Existence, the Trinity, and God's Love; and How to Have a Personal Relationship with God

Link to ebook: https://www.amazon.com/dp/B082RNRVBF

The Universe is Not Dying: A unified physics theory explaining the mysteries of dimensions, space, strings, matter, energy, light, time, particle spin, wave formation, black holes, quasars, and the energy-matter cycle

Link to ebook: https://www.amazon.com/dp/B083DP6MVC

Drs. Jordan's Fables: Book One

Link to ebook: https://www.amazon.com/dp/B084FZH9DY

Drs. Jordan's Fables: Book Two

Link to ebook: **https://www.amazon.com/dp/B084WNG8W8**

Thus Says The Lord God

Link to ebook: **https://www.amazon.com/dp/B085BLSH23**

Drs. Jordan's Fables: Book Three

Link to ebook: **https://www.amazon.com/dp/B085QBWXHP**

Thus Say The Biblical Prophets And Apostles: Volume I

Link to ebook: **https://www.amazon.com/dp/B08689G32J**

Thus Say The Biblical Prophets And Apostles: Volume II

Link to ebook: **https://www.amazon.com/dp/B086JFY6KB**

What Is A Good Husband?

Link to ebook: **https://www.amazon.com/dp/B0871T5ZQQ**

The Lost Books Of Wisdom

Link to ebook: https://www.amazon.com/dp/B087BF3WV6

The Ancient Wisdom Of The West

Link to ebook: https://www.amazon.com/dp/B087Q566F7

Christian Faith In The Age Of Disbelief And Unbelief: Attaining, Growing And Maintaining The Christian Faith Needed For Salvation

Link to ebook: https://www.amazon.com/dp/B0881J6LM3

Drs. Jordan's Proverbial Wit And Wisdom From The Animal Kingdom

Link to ebook: https://www.amazon.com/dp/B088F6RSQ7

DRS. JORDAN's WHATS, WHYS and HOWS RATIONALES of CARDIOLOGY BOOK ONE: CARDIOVASCULAR SYSTEM

Link to ebook: https://www.amazon.com/dp/B089GJH86C

Many peer reviewed journal articles